KIM AND JERRY BRODEY
CAN YOU HEAR MY VOICE
TEACHER'S GUIDE

Anti-bias
Songs and classroom activities
For Kindergarten through Grade 6

By Kim and Jerry Brodey
and Ruth-Ann MacKinnon
Illustrations by Jerry Brodey

Peace is not an object found by chance –
It is the result of equality between (people).

Anonymous mural
Oruro, Bolivia

TABLE OF CONTENTS

ACKNOWLEDGEMENTS

This Teacher's Guide has been a collaboration from the beginning between us, our friend and colleague Ruth-Ann MacKinnon and many other people we consulted who are working in the area of anti-bias education.

As we created the music and activities for Can You Hear My Voice, we were profoundly aware of our own limitations as white, middle class members of a racist, sexist, classist society. It has been an ongoing learning experience for us and we are indebted to the following people for offering us the wisdom of their voices:

Chandra Budhu, coordinator, Community Action on Violence Against Women Project, YWCA;

Tom Edwards, vice-principal, Market Lane Public School, Toronto Board of Education;

Philip Fernandez, programme trainer, Frontier College;

Patricia Hays, race relations consultant, North York Board of Education;

Victoria Moon Joyce, artist, writer, Outward Bound leader;

Mona Katawne, human resource consultant, Zebra Group, Winnipeg;

Ann Lacey, writer, teacher, Downtown Alternative School, Toronto Board of Education;

Hari Lalla, coordinator, race relations and multiculturalism, Toronto Board of Education;

Pria Muzumdar, artist, educator, founder of Funcepts;

Myra Novogrodsky, coordinator, women's studies and labour studies, Toronto Board of Education;

Yasmeen Saddiqui, writer, educator, partner in Funcepts

Deborah Sinclair, activist, trainer in the area of violence against women and children;

Nancy Steele, teacher, Horizon Alternative School, Toronto Board of Education;

Karen Thomas, teacher, North York Board of Education

– Kim and Jerry Brodey

A NOTE TO TEACHERS

One day we heard a group of boys taunting some girls in a Toronto schoolyard, making offensive remarks about skin colour and genitals. The girls didn't respond – this was part of playing around with their classmates. Neither the boys nor the girls knew how to talk to each other in a respectful way. At their young age they were already being propelled onto paths of behaviour dictated by our racist, sexist society. Wasn't there a way for these children to communicate with each other in a more authentic way? Where were *their* voices?

This project is our way of helping children find those voices by challenging prejudices and celebrating our diverse and common stories. We start with the individual, because children have to value themselves before they can value others. Building self-esteem, and a pride in one's culture and ethnic background, comes first. The second step is to help children expand their experience so they are comfortable with people of all kinds. The more they know about each other, the more they will understand and respect each other.

We hope the activities in this book will help your students appreciate that we do not all look, feel or act the same.

And finally, we want to hear your voices, too. Please write with your comments, stories and new ideas.

ABOUT THE ORDER
This book is a companion to the recording Can You Hear My Voice. You will find that the order of titles on the tape is different from the order in the book. Here's why: The songs and poetry on the tape are ordered to create a varied musical flow. In the book, the songs and activites are ordered in a developmental way, beginning with communication skills and building on those to prepare for later subjects.

We encourage you, however, to use the songs, poetry and activities in whatever order makes sense for your classroom.

CREATING A 'SAFE CIRCLE'

This book offers many suggestions for classroom discussions. We believe that encouraging children to explore their ideas and feelings out loud is a fundamental part of anti-bias education. Telling children what they should be thinking breeds resistance. Listening to children fosters self- esteem.

Most of the discussions we suggest can take place in daily informal exchanges in the classroom. However, it can be very valuable to establish what we call a 'safe circle' in which children feel free to talk about sensitive, sometimes even painful subjects, in the knowledge they will be listened to with compassion.

The safe circle works best under clearly understood conditions that honour confidentiality, trust and equal time. It can include the whole class but might work better with groups of eight to ten. Safe circle could start with a ceremony, such as lighting a candle to symbolize each individual's inner spirit. This differentiates the exercise from routine classroom discussions. Here are some more guidelines:

START by talking about non-threatening topics (what did you do for summer vacation?) until group members are comfortable with more intimate thoughts (when was a time you did something you wish you hadn't?).

SIT IN A CIRCLE at the same height. Everyone is equal in a circle – it has no front or back. It's OK to sit on chairs, but don't sit around a table because having something between you can block discussion. Bring yourself to the circle and nothing else.

DON'T ALLOW anybody to dominate the discussion. If it seems that some people take up more than their share of time, you may need to develop a system to keep track of time.

SPEAK in turn, moving around the circle. Those who have nothing to contribute are free to say, "I pass." In some circles, holding your hands together on your lap indicates you are ready to speak. If your hands are apart, you are not called upon. Coaxing a student to speak might make them feel they have an expectation to live up to. They are participating just by being in the circle.

LISTEN without interrupting or probing. Some circles use a "talking stick" to make it clear whose turn it is. Only the person holding the talking stick may speak. Instead of a stick, you could use a smooth rock or even a special object such as a teddy bear for younger children.

RESIST the temptation to always fill silence with words. It might be necessary to wait in silence for somebody to speak.

We think the song We Are The Voice Of The Earth is perfect for closing circle time. It needs no accompaniment. Just hold hands and sing.

A program of circle discussion topics for all age groups has been developed by the Human Development Program. For more information about their book, Grounds for Growth, see Resources on Page 74.

WE ARE THE VOICE OF THE EARTH

Music/Lyrics by Jerry Brodey
© 1992 JERRY BRODEY (Socan)

We are the voice of the earth,
Hear the wind saying.
We turn around to the sun
And circle it changing.

CHORUS:
We are the voice of the earth,
Rising up, rising up. (repeat)

We are the voice of our times,
Earth and moon dancing.
There is the healing that comes,
In the circle we're singing.

(chorus)

We hear a voice in ourselves,
Friends we are calling.
We struggle, finding our way,
The circle is changing.

(chorus)

WE ARE THE VOICE OF THE EARTH

Discussion

Children who are comfortable with their own feelings are better equipped to understand the feelings of others and to treat each other with fairness and respect.

Feelings are neither right nor wrong, good nor bad. They simply are;

One person's feelings in any given situation might not be the same as another's;

Feelings are changeable. They come and go with our thoughts, the time of day, our health, the weather;

Anger is usually a signal that a tender feeling has not been expressed;

At discussion time, ask students, "how do you feel when...
It rains.
it's sunny.
you are late for school.
you have to stop watching TV in the middle of a show.
a classmate compliments your work.
the teacher compliments your work.
you are singing a song.
someone gives you a gift.
you give a gift to someone.
you are in a room full of people you don't know.
you are in a room full of people you do know.
you did something you shouldn't have.
you did something you used to be afraid of.
you tried and tried at something and succeeded.
you play with your things at home, alone for an hour.
your friend asks you to go bicycle riding.
somebody picks on you.

Now discuss:

does everyone in the group feel the same about everything?

Can you feel more than one feeling at the same time?

What are examples of feelings you like to have?

What are examples of feelings you don't like to have?

What can you do about feelings you don't like to have? (talk about them)

Is it ever difficult to tell the truth?

Activities

These exercises are designed to help students identify their feelings and develop a vocabulary to express them. Communication skills do not come without practice.

1. FEELING VOCABULARY (All levels)

frustrated	confident	tense	comforted
dependent	serious	discouraged	anxious
sunshiny	bored	cheerful	embarrassed
excited	afraid	happy	impatient
powerless	jealous	carefree	nervous
proud	capable	relieved	ashamed
surprised	guilty	awed	affectionate
bossy	nasty	scared	cantankerous
wilful	loving	frisky	giddy
independent	calm	little	misunderstood
insecure	courageous	uptight	lonely
pleased	inadequate	defiant	empathetic
envious	strong	thankful	silly
hopeful	honest	respectful	brave

Use the list of words above for some of the following activities, according to the ages and abilities in your class:

Find pairs of opposites in the list.

Find pairs of words that have similar meanings.

Put the words in alphabetical order.

Add more feeling words to the list.

Make a feeling-word dictionary.

Make up a crossword puzzle using five feeling words.

Have a spelling test using feeling words.

2. PUPPET SHOWS (Kindergarden to Grade 3)

Make up and perform short puppet plays using feeling words in the title. For example:

"The Frightened Giraffe"

"Sadness at a Mill Street Birthday Party"

"Carlotta's Proud Day"

3. TV TITLES (Grades 4 to 6)

Make up names and summaries of television shows using a feeling word in the title. For example:

"The Bored Baboon" – a young zoo inhabitant can't stand the monotony and gets into trouble.

"The Girl Who Was Never Surprised" – Rivka's friends prepare a secret party for her. Will she find out what they are up to?

4. "I" MESSAGES (Grades 4 to 6)

The object here is to teach students to communicate their own feelings. Too often, we blame other people when something goes wrong ("You're making too much noise!") instead of informing them of our reactions ("I'm feeling irritable about the noise level because I can't concentrate on my work").

Blaming can lead to defensiveness and hurt feelings ("I am not making too much noise!") while informing encourages co-operative behaviour ("Oh, I'm sorry, I'll try to keep it down").

The trick is to begin sentences with the word "I". You might be surprised how effective this simple technique can be.

Make photocopies of the following page to distribute to the class. Because the nature of the questions might lead students to make personal revelations, it is important to respect their privacy. Students don't have to put their names on the papers and don't have to share the work with other classmates.

There are no right or wrong answers.

"I" MESSAGES WORK SHEET

Use feeling words to fill in the blanks in the following sentences:

1. I feel _____ when everybody is talking because I can't concentrate on my work.

2. I feel _____ when I finish reading a book because I know I will start another.

3. I feel _____ when my friend yells at me because I think she/he doesn't like me.

4. I feel _____ when I am asked to help another student with math because I know the teacher appreciates my work.

5. I feel _____ when another student brings a new tape recorder to school because I wish I could have one like it.

6. I feel _____ when I see my classmate being bullied by bigger children because I know it's not fair.

Fill in the blanks in the following sentences:

1. I feel tense when I have to do something in class because_____
_____.

2. I feel excited when it's my birthday because_____
_____.

3. I feel carefree at recess because_____
_____.

4. I feel impatient in gym class because _____.

5. I feel frustrated when I am writing because _____.

6. I feel comforted when I visit my friend because _____

_____.

Now make up your own "I messages" using this formula:

I feel _____ when _____ because _____.

CAN YOU HEAR MY VOICE

Music/Lyrics by Jerry Brodey

A child is crying — Can you hear my voice?
He's tired and hungry — Can you hear my voice?
She needs a little tenderness — Can you hear my voice?

CHORUS:
LA LA LA LA...

I want to shout to the mountain — Can you hear my voice?
I feel joy in the blue sky — Can you hear my voice?
My homeland is calling — Can you hear my voice?

(chorus)

When I'm feeling frightened — Can you hear my voice?
When my knees are trembling — Can you hear my voice?
When my heart is sinking — Can you hear my voice?

(chorus)

BRIDGE:
Sing your song
Sing it out strong (repeat)

Will you be my brother? — Can you hear my voice?
Will you be my sister? — Can you hear my voice?
I've been so lonely — Can you hear my voice?

(chorus)

Take a moment to celebrate — Can you hear my voice?
With you I want to celebrate — Can you hear my voice?
Take a moment to celebrate — Can you hear my voice?

(chorus)

CAN YOU HEAR MY VOICE?

Discussion

It is as important to be a good listener as it is to be a good talker. In your circle, ask:
>Have you ever been talking and the other person wasn't listening?
>How did it feel?
>Has it ever happened that you said one thing and the person
>thought you meant something else? What did that feel like?
>What are some effective ways to attract someone's attention?
>What should you not do to attract someone's attention?
>What should you do if you are not ready to listen to someone?

Activities

1. LISTENING THAT WORKS/LISTENING THAT DOESN'T WORK
(All levels)

First, brainstorm about listening behaviour. What shows a person is really listening? This can be looking at the speaker, head nodding, making comments such as 'I understand' or smiling if the speaker says something funny. What shows a person is not really listening? This can be fidgeting, watching another activity, reading a book, not responding, and so on.

Now, divide the class into pairs. A and B sit facing each other. A talks for one minute about a favorite book and B acts out listening that doesn't work. Then A talks for one minute and B demonstrates attentive listening. Reverse positions so B is the speaker and A the listener.

Talk about what both examples feel like. Did you know that in some cultures it is considered rude to look into the eyes of the person speaking to you? Point out that "eye-contact listening" is *one* way of being attentive – not the only, or "correct" way.

2. BODY LANGUAGE (Kindergarden to Grade 3)

Demonstrate examples of different facial expressions and body language and ask students to guess what you are feeling – happy, sad, frightened, excited or embarrassed. Give students a sheet of paper with four ovals drawn on it and ask them to draw one of each: a sad face, happy face, frightened face, embarrassed face.

3. MASK MAKING (Kindergarten to Grade 3)

For each child, glue a popsicle stick to a paper plate to make a mask. Students then design one of the following faces on their mask: happy, embarrassed, frightened or sad. Use markers, crayons, colored paper, fabric scraps, yarn and whatever materials are available. Do not cut out eyes because they can be one of the most expressive features. When you talk about your masks later, ask:

What do you think that person is thinking?
Imagine something that would make them feel like that.
What might they say?
What would you say to them?

4. BROKEN TELEPHONE (Kindergarten to Grade 3)

This game works best in a circle with 9 to 12 children. Each participant has a chance to whisper a phrase to the person on his or her right. The saying is passed on in whispers from player to player until the last person says it out loud. Compare the final phrase to the original one.

Here are some phrases you can try:

Saskatoon is in Saskatchewan.
Butterflies flutter by better.
Mary, oh Mary open the gate.
Our radishes get redder by the hour.

Now try "Fixed telephone" and see if the message can be transmitted accurately if everyone tries really hard.

5. IT'S HOW YOU SAY IT (Grades 4 to 6)

It's not just what you say, it's also how you say it that communicates your feelings. Discuss with students: Has it happened that someone is smiling at you but you can tell they are angry? How can you tell? Tone of voice and physical stance send messages, just as words do. As an exercise, concentrate on communicating using your words, your tone of voice and your stance. Take a phrase such as "close the door" and have the children say it in ways that express these different feelings: anger, impatience, friendliness, affection, excitement, fear, fatigue, happiness, patience, confidence, relief, courage.

BABY IN THE BELLY

Music/Lyrics by Jerry Brodey
© 1992 JERRY BRODEY (Socan)

Baby in the belly,
Trying to come out. (repeat)
First breath in and
Sun is out. (repeat)

Baby in belly,
Trying to come out. (repeat)
Second breath in
Hooray she's out. (repeat)

Like a seed in the soil
With the rainfall too. (repeat)
This plant is growing
Just like you. (repeat)

1-2-3-4-5-6-7, 8-9-10
10 years old... 100 years old
Our spirit lives on and on and on.

Baby, child, old woman, old man,
Each one part of a special clan.
Into this world we're born, we live and we die;
In our short time all we can do is try.

(repeat verses 1 - 3)

BABY IN THE BELLY

Discussion

LISTENING to this song in the class will probably generate questions like: "Where did I come from?" Be informative in a matter-of-fact way and explain that being born is a natural process and, indeed, one of the few things everybody in the whole world has done. Children love talking about when they were babies. Discuss:

How do babies eat before they are born?

Do babies breathe before they are born?

Does anybody remember being a baby?

What's your earliest memory?

What day of the week were you born on?

What was the first word you said?

What was your favourite food when you were a baby?

Why are some people born boys and some girls?

Why are some people born with brown hair and others with red hair? brown skin, beige skin? blue eyes, brown eyes?

In what ways do you look like your mother?

In what ways do you look like your father?

If any of your students are adopted by families of a different racial background, you can ask the students and their families in advance how they wish you to explain their background so they don't feel unprepared and perhaps uncomfortable during the class discussion.

Activities

1. BABY PICTURE POSTER (All levels)

Ask students to each bring one of their baby pictures from home. Make a poster using all the photos, with each baby identified. You might want to have children write captions for their pictures, imagining what they were thinking at the time the camera clicked. Display the poster in the classroom.

2. SKIN COLOUR – NOT BLACK AND WHITE (All levels)

Sometimes finding a starting point can be the most challenging part of teaching a subject as delicate as racial characteristics. Announcing to the class, "Now we are going to talk about skin colour," is bound to make everyone uncomfortable.

Listening to the song Baby In The Belly opens the door to talking with children in Kindergarten to Grade 3 about birth and inherited characteristics. For Grades 4 to 6, the song Moving In A Big Sea provides a starting point for a discussion about individual differences.

Talking about racial characteristics is an important step in fostering positive attitudes about people of different backgrounds. But if only a small percentage of the class represents a certain race, they are liable to feel singled out during a discussion of skin colour. Prepare them beforehand by telling them what to expect.

Ask students to compare skin colour with each other. Are any two exactly the same? Probably not, because the fact is, we all have skin that is some variation of brown and even brothers and sisters in one family can have differing skin colour.

Does anyone think they are black or white? Obviously, nobody is pure black or pure white. These colours are not just misnomers, they also help perpetuate racism because they have so many biased connotations. In the movies, the "good guy" always wears white, while the "bad guy" wears black. If you are in a "black mood," you don't feel happy.

With your class, make a list of words that more accurately describe skin tones.

3. SKIN COLOUR – HAND TREE (Kindergarten to Grade 3)

Another approach to the subject of skin colour is to have students experiment with mixing paint colours to arrive at their own skin colour.

Students then trace the shape of their hand on a piece of construction paper and colour the traced hand with the paint they have mixed. When the paint is dry, cut out the hands. Make the trunk and branches of a tree in brown paper and pin it on the bulletin board. Tack the painted hands on as leaves.

Talk about why there are so many different shades of skin colour.

About 100,000 years ago, there were three or four pure races in the world. Now, there are some 2,000 different kinds of people, so many that we don't even have names for them all.

Skin colour (as well as eye and hair colour) are determined by the amount of the pigment melanin. Everybody has some of this pigment in their skin and the concentration varies according to race for geographic reasons.

The skin of races traditionally in hot, tropical regions (such as Africa) contains more melanin to protect the body from harmful sun rays (although people of colour can get sunburnt). People of northern European ancestry have lighter brown skin to allow more of the sun's rays to penetrate since their climate is cold.

There are also logical reasons behind peoples' different shapes and sizes that go back hundreds and hundreds of years. Tall, thin bodies stay cooler while short, wider bodies retain warmth. People of Asian ancestry have a larger upper eyelid to protect their eyeballs from the dust.

4. BIRTHDAY GARDEN (Kindergarten to Grade 3)

Just as we grow each year, so do plants. Our ancient ancestors knew the sun helped things grow. They held ceremonies to help bring about good harvest. We are like plants, needing encouragement to grow in healthy, bountiful ways. Using different colours of construction paper, cut out shapes of flowers: lilies, roses, tulips, daffodils, daisies, petunias, violets and any others you can imagine. On each one write the birthdate of a child in the class. Display this "birthday garden" on a bulletin board in the classroom. As each birthday occurs, take the child's flower off and sing, from the song Baby in the Belly:

> *Like a seed in the soil*
> *With the rainfall too*
> *This plant is growing*
> *Just like you*

5. PAPER DOLL SELF PORTRAITS (Kindergarten to Grade 3)

Start by discussing shapes of body parts. Have students hold a circle up to show faces are not round, they are oval. Using mirrors and rulers, measure different features. How far is it from your eyes to the top of your head? How far from your eyes to the bottom of your head? Where are your ears in relation to your eyes? How does the length of your torso compare to the length of your legs – longer or shorter? Are your legs longer than your arms?

Once you have discussed proportions, cut out heads, torsos, arms and legs and assemble them into paper dolls that approximate the same proportions. Draw faces and use paper, fabric scraps, ribbon, buttons, and any other materials you have on hand to dress dolls.

We recommend an educational workshop called All Together Now Canada by Funcepts which allows students to explore physical characteristics through art. See resources at the back of this book for more information.

WALKING DOWN THE ROAD

Music/Lyrics by Jerry Brodey
© 1992 JERRY BRODEY (Socan)

*Walking down the road
Going to visit, going to visit.
Walking down the road, going to visit my friends.
Carlos, Kuldip, Laura, Filippo.
Walking down the road, going to visit my friends.*

Walking down the road.

*Running through the cornstalks
Going to visit, going to visit.
Running through the cornstalks, going to visit my friends.
Veda, Asher, Joan, Abdul.
Running through the cornstalks, going to visit my friends.*

*Running through the cornstalks
Walking down the road.*

*Climbing up the mountain...
Markus, Coco, Amaral, Sophie
Climbing up the mountain, going to visit my friends.*

*Climbing up the mountain
Running through the cornstalks
Walking down the road.*

*Digging in the earth...
Merike, Micah, Lilly, Guiseppe.
Digging in the earth, going to visit my friends.*

Digging in the earth
Climbing up the mountain
Running through the cornstalks
Walking down the road.

Swimming in the river...
Lucy, Geezis, Mongo, Milly.
Swimming in the river, going to visit my friends.

Swimming in the river
Digging in the earth
Climbing up the mountain
Running through the cornstalks
Walking down the road.

Rolling down the mountain...
Khoshnaw, William, Sunyat, Ben...
Finally, here I am playing with my friends.

WALKING DOWN THE ROAD

Discussion

A few days on the subject of names can be a good entry point with a new group. Our names are fundamental symbols of our identities and honoring a name is a way of affirming that individual. Here are some questions you can ask:

How did your parents choose your name?

Did you have a naming ceremony?

What is the difference between a family name and a given name?

Not all cultures follow the same tradition for passing
on family names.

What are some examples?

Do you have more than one given name name?

Do you have more than one family name?

Is your family name your first name or your last name?

Do you know anyone else with the same name?

Do you know how to say your name in another language?

Some names have meanings, does yours?

Do you have a nickname? If so, do you like it or not?

What would the class be like if everyone had the same name?

If students in the class represent many ethnic and/or religious groups, this is a way to learn from each other. If, however, most or all of the students have similar ethnic/religious backgrounds, it would be valuable to teach them that, for example in China a person's given name is usually their second name while their first name is usually their family name. Many Spanish children receive the maiden name of their mother as well as their father's surname.

Activities

1. NAME ART (All levels)

Draw it, paint it, sculpt it! As an art project, have students draw their name and decorate it. Or, have them make a plasticine sculpture or plaque of their name. Display the works of art in the classroom.

> Reserve a special display space for each student in the class. Their name art can identify this space and other creative projects they complete can be exhibited in their personal gallery all year long!

2. NAME SONG - 1 (Kindergarten to Grade 3)

Sing Walking Down The Road together. Once the class is familiar with the tune, add verses to include the names of the children in your class. Make up your own journeys, too. Add actions to the song. Sing it again.

3. NAME SONG - 2 (Kindergarten to Grade 3)

Stand in a circle and take turns singing your names. Begin by getting a clapping rhythm going together. One by one each person steps toward the centre of the circle and makes up a melody and an action to go with his or her name. Everyone else repeats the music and action.

> Be comfortable with students' names before beginning this exercise. Children are very sensitive about their names and like to have them pronounced correctly. Mispronounced names can be used for teasing.

4. NAME STORIES (Grades 4 to 6)

Name stories are fascinating, whether you describe a naming ceremony, tell about the aunt who is your namesake or recall the amusing way you mispronounced your name when you were just learning to talk. Some people have poignant stories about immigrants forced to change their names on arrival in Canada. Others can bring in pictures of the famous person they were named after.

Ask students for their name stories. This can be done orally in the circle or as a written assignment. Make sure students read their stories out loud to the class because this is one of the ways they can learn about each other.

5. TEAM NAMES (Grades 4 to 6)

If you were a soccer coach, would you call your team the Pussy Cats? Why or why not? Whoever named the Washington Redskins, Atlanta Braves or Edmonton Eskimos probably didn't realize their choice was influenced by the stereotype of natives as fierce, warlike people. How do you think indigenous people feel about there being a team named the Redskins? What are some other examples of team names that perpetuate stereotypes? What is the name of the team at your school? Could it be offensive to any group? Create an imaginary league and think up team names that do not trivialize a cultural group.

IN THE HOUSE WHERE I LIVE

Music/Lyrics by Jerry Brodey
© 1992 JERRY BRODEY (Socan)

On the first floor lives a very special lady,
A woman so colourful, bright and bold.
She is an artist, a dancer,
Her words are like wooden chimes.
There's grey hair underneath
The wig she always wears.

Altogether her three children,
Including me, a neighbour;
We play hide and seek underneath the beds.
This mother sits at the kitchen table,
Sipping Chinese tea
Her loving friends come to visit her and see.

CHORUS:
Family — in the house where I live.
Family — so much that they would give;
Neighbours I find, different kinds
Of family.

Three floors up live two men,
Two dogs, two cats, a parakeet,
A child who whistles and she sings.
They are cheerful and kind,
Sometimes we would dine
Around their table, this family and mine.

(chorus)

There was a man and woman, never did we meet.
They lived above us, for the shortest time of all.
I won't forget the nights
As I would try to sleep;
I heard her cries and shouts,
Then they began to weep.

Next to me live the Bozaks,
A mother, father and the twins,
Grandparents who came to them by boat.
The story's told that the only thing they could bring,
As they fled their distant home,
Were two family pictures underneath their old worn coats.

(chorus)

IN THE HOUSE WHERE I LIVE

Discussion

This song is a perfect introduction to talking about families. We know that families come in all shapes and sizes and discussing the differences and similarities helps children appreciate individual family styles. Children might wish to explore the fourth verse in the song which acknowledges, sadly, that not all families are happy.

Listen to the song together and then talk about the different types of families you know.

Does anyone know families like the ones in the song?

Does anyone have the same number of people in their house as their neighbours do?

How many people are in your family?

Do you know a family with no children?

Is anybody an oldest child? youngest? only? twin?

Who takes care of the children in your family? grandparent? father? mother? older child?

How many generations are living together in your family?

Does anybody have two families that they divide their time between?

Who does most of the cooking in your family?

What is mealtime like at your house?

What makes a family a family?

What do all families have in common?

Activities

1. FAMILY POSTERS (All levels)

Have each child bring from home one or two family photos that can be used on a poster. If this is not possible, have children make drawings of the people in their families. Have each child make a poster with words and pictures that tell about themselves and their families. Display the posters in the classroom.

2. FAMILY STORIES (All levels)

Divide the class into groups of four and ask each group to imagine four families. For younger children do this activity in one group. Each family must have a different configuration from the others. The groups must create stories of how each family came to be and write a short story for each that describes their lives.

Create puppets and act out a family scene such as dinner, bed time or Sunday afternoon.

FALL 1992
Ronnie + Gramps   16 MONTHS
                   72 YEARS

3. APARTMENT ART (All levels)

Using the family stories your class wrote, create an apartment complex! This art project requires:

> an empty cereal box for each child
> paper
> scissors
> ruler
> pencils and crayons or markers
> construction paper or paint
> glue

Write and illustrate the family stories on 4 booklets, each using two pieces of paper 10cm X 15 cm (4 inches X 6 inches) folded and stapled in the middle. Design the cover of each booklet as a window. When you open the booklet create different family scenes. Leave the back cover of the book blank.

Use paint or construction paper to cover the cereal box. This is the apartment building. Glue the four booklets onto one side – two side by side on the "ground floor" and two above on the "second floor" so they look like four windows. Use crayons or markers to make a front door, flower boxes, and any other design features imaginable.

As each student finishes their apartment building, have them present it to the class.

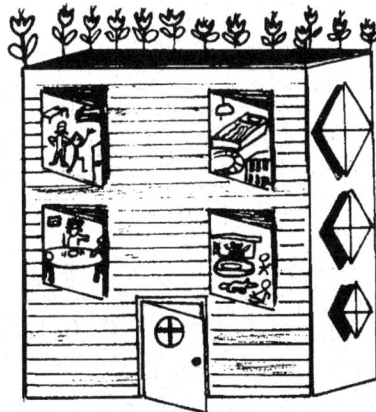

4. BREAD, BREAD, BREAD (All levels)

The book Globalchild, Multicultural Resources for Young Children, by Maureen Cech, is a rich source of classroom activities that bring up similarities among cultures. It points out that snack time is a chance to share ideas and a taste of another culture through broadening food experiences.

Put a variety of breads on your snack plate and "slice them, stuff them, spread them, dip them, toast them, or cut them with cookie cutters to make interesting shapes."

Here are some of the breads you may want to use:

Bagels (Jewish)
Baguette (French)
Bannock (early Canadian)
Bran bread
Challah (Jewish)
Chapati (Indian)
Christonomo (Italian)
Cornbread
Corn pone (Central Amer.)
Croissants (French)
Datebread
Fry bread (Navajo)
Gingerbread
Injera (Ethiopian)
Irish soda bread
Kamaj (Palestinian)

Klaben (German)
Knackbröd (German)
Laufabrod (Icelandic)
Matzo (Jewish)
Muffins
Nan (Indian)
Pita (Middle Eastern)
Popovers
Potato Bread
Pumpernickel
Pumpkin bread
Raisin bread
Roti (Caribbean/East Indian)
Rye bread
Steamed buns (Chinese)
Tortillas (Mexican)

5. HOUSES AROUND THE WORLD (Grades 4 to 6)

As a research project, learn about housing around the world. Draw pictures and make models of homes in other countries. Try to imagine what it would be like to live in a thatch hut on the banks of the Amazon River or in a stone dwelling high in the Andes mountains. What kind of housing is built in Japan? in Mexico? in Bali? Why?

> As part of the research for this project, show photographs of high-rise apartments and upper-class housing in the large cities of South America and Indonesia to illustrate the diversity of housing within each country, too.

MOVING IN A BIG SEA

Music/Lyrics by Jerry Brodey
© 1992 JERRY BRODEY (Socan)

I've heard you calling me names,
You say my nose is too long.
Don't you know where this treasure comes from?
Far off places, for all our faces,
Scenic and curvy,
For people like me.

CHORUS:
My thinking gets muddled,
My head all befuddled,
Moving in a big sea.
We're finding our own space,
Creating a new place — together,
Moving in a big sea
Of diversity.

I've seen you walk down the street —
To me you're huge, with muscles made of concrete.
I feel overpowered by you;
When you stand above me,
I'm much smaller,
You take advantage,
Because you're taller!

(chorus)

What if we were laundry together?
Hanging out in the breeze.
Airing all our differences;
I could be flowered shirts,
You — pants or mini-skirts,
Hankies or bikini briefs.

(chorus)

MOVING IN A BIG SEA

Discussion

Here is an opportunity to illustrate to students that "different" doesn't automatically mean "better" or "worse". Questions to discuss:

If you like apples, does that mean you don't like oranges? why?

If you like blue shirts does that mean you don't like red shirts?

If you like the shape of your own nose, does that mean you don't like the shape of someone else's nose? Why?

When two things are different, does that mean one is better than the other?

Is a square better than or different from a rectangle?

Is the number 3 better than or different from the number 5?

Can a person with long hair have something in common with a person with short hair? What are some examples of things they share?

Can a tall person have something in common with a short person? What are some examples?

Is there anything bad about being different?

Is there a "typical" Canadian?

What is good about being different?

Activities

1. MEETING BETWEEN GRADES (All levels)

This is designed as a joint project between younger children (Kindergarden to Grade 3) and older children (Grade 4 to 6). The idea is for each group to make a presentation to the other about the advantages and disadvantages of their respective age groups. They can do this using prepared speeches, skits, music, pictures or whatever works. Leave time for discussion after the presentations and then serve cookies and juice.

Here are some ideas to consider:

What do you like about being old/young?

What do yout not like about being old/young?

Younger children: do you think the older children understand you?

Older children: do you think the younger children understand you?

How does it feel to be in an argument with someone older/younger?

Do you ever feel you have to give in to someone because they are younger? How does that feel?

Do you ever feel you have to do what someone else says because they are older than you? How does that feel?

Do you ever feel that a baby or younger child should do what you say because you are older than them?

What can we do together even though we're different ages?

2. STICKS AND STONES (All levels)

"Sticks and stones can break my bones but names can never hurt me." Most of us know from experience that this chant is a cover-up. Names can and do hurt. Talk about teasing:

Has anybody ever teased you in a way that made you laugh?

Has anybody ever teased you in a way you didn't like?

Why do people tease other people?

Why is teasing acceptable sometimes and not other times?

Do you like to be teased?

How can you make someone stop teasing you?

Do you like to tease others?

How can you tell if someone likes your teasing or not?

As a writing exercise, have students think of a new way to finish the phrase "Sticks and stones can break my bones ..."

3. GIVING AND ACCEPTING COMPLIMENTS (All levels)

Tell students that for the next 10 minutes it's "Compliment Time" and the ony talking allowed is to give or receive a compliment. Make sure they know how to receive a compliment graciously, without denying it or belittling themselves in any way. (This can be a way to change the atmosphere in a classroom where one or more students are feeling picked on.)

4. LANGUAGE OF FEATURES (All levels)

Certain ways of describing people's physical characteristics can be interpreted as hurtful, so it is important to develop a clear vocabulary of features. Many dark-skinned people prefer to be called people of colour. The term "black" is not only inaccurate – we are all a tone of brown somewhere between black and white – it also carries with it some negative connotations. Think of a black mood or a dark day.

Other terms referring to physical features have been used derogatorily so often that they are no longer descriptive, such as "big-nose", "flat-nose" or "slant-eyes". A nose with a high bridge might look large but it isn't necessarily bigger than a nose with a low bridge.

Make a list of terms that are OK and terms that are Not OK.
Here's a beginning:

OK	NOT OK
almond-shaped eyes	slant-eyes
woman (for someone over 18)	girl (for someone over 18)
mentally challenged	retarded
disabled	crippled

Opinions will differ. For example, some of the First Nations people of Canada like to be called Indians; some do not. The key is to respect the terminology of the person concerned.

5. WHO AM I THINKING OF? (Grades 4 to 6)

In this game, a student writes down the name of another student in the class and then gives the class 3 hints so they can guess whose name is on the paper. The student must follow the list (above) of terms that are OK to describe physical features.

6. UNDERSTANDING PREJUDICE (Grades 4 to 6)

Prejudice is an attitude formed without knowledge. It is judging something before you are informed about it. Tell students you are going to give them a vegetable snack. Ask them to write down whether or not they expect to like it. Then give them pieces of carrot cake. Was everybody's prediction correct? Why or why not? How is this an example of prejudice?

Just as one ingredient in the carrot cake doesn't constitute the finished dessert, one aspect of a person doesn't characterize that person. We can't judge a person by their skin colour, hairdo, clothes, size, strength or any other single feature.

Has anybody experienced any examples of prejudice? How do people become prejudiced? Do prejudiced people want everyone to look the same?

MAJOR BOWLES

Music/Lyrics by Jerry Brodey
© 1992 JERRY BRODEY (Socan)

CHORUS:
Major Bowles, famous for his strange
And wondrous shows.
Never have you seen such spectacles,
Like eccentric Major Bowles.

The zoo keeper's daughter gargled with salt water
While she sang her tune.
Standing on her head, we watched her all turn red,
Under the lights, what a delight, what a night.

(chorus)

There's the girl from Tonawanda,
Whose dancing anaconda used a hoola hoop.
What about the guy who turned his face inside out,
Look at his lips upon his ears, listen to the cheers.

(chorus)

BRIDGE:
Every year people come from all the world over,
To see the unbelievable to hear the inconceivable
To see what they thought could not be done.

Would you believe the rubberman?
He squished himself inside a can and rolled himself off stage.
How far will people go, to get attention, I don' t know.
But soon we'll see, Saturday night with Major Bowles.

(chorus)

MAJOR BOWLES

Discussion

Here's a chance to let your imagination run wild! Encourage students to think freely by asking them these questions:

If you could wear whatever you wanted to school, what would you wear?

If you could go to any country you wanted, where would you go?

If you were in an orchestra, which instrument would you play?

If you were in the circus, what act would you want to do?

If you could be an animal, which animal would you be?

If you could be a plant, which plant would you be?

Activities

1. CRAZY TALENT SHOW (All levels)

Performing can be a way of getting attention in a positive way. Organize a production in which each student has a chance to show off an individual skill – the more fun the better. No doubt your students will have individual specialities they will be happy to perform. To get them thinking, use this list of ideas for acts:

jump rope	juggling	magic tricks
joke telling	shadow puppets	imaginary pet tricks
whistling	speaking fast	mime
lip sync	singing	balancing
puppet show	dancing	drumming
hula hoop	poetry	kazoo

Students should have equal time for their acts and remember that this should not become a competition. The idea is that everybody is special.

Make posters and props for the show, and invite families and other classes to see the great spectacle.

2. MAJOR BOWLES DRAWINGS (All levels)

Play the song Major Bowles in the class, telling students they will be asked to draw characters from the talent show. After they have drawn and coloured one of the performers, ask students to make up a character and draw it.

3. MIXED-UP DAY (Kindergarden to Grade 3)

April Fool's day is a good time to schedule this fun activity. Students wear shirts and pants back-to-front, have recess at the beginning of the day, have morning activities in the afternoon and vice versa. Of course it's more fun if the teacher wears a goofy outfit, too.

4. ECCENTRIC vs CONVENTIONAL (Grades 4 to 6)

Word list: eccentric, weird, zany, conventional, normal, ordinary

Discuss definitions of the words in the word list and then ask students to answer all of the following questions about each word:

a. have you ever felt _____
b. did you like feeling _____
c. write a sentence using the word _____

5. MAJOR BOWLES BIOGRAPHY (Grades 4 to 6)

Play the song Major Bowles for the class and then ask them to invent a two-page biography of Major Bowles. Here are some questions they might answer in their biography. What kind of a childhood did Major Bowles have? What were his parents like? Did he have brothers and sisters? Did he have many friends? What did he do for fun? What did he do when he was sad? What kind of a school did he go to? What people did he look up to? What are some events of his life that he'll never forget?

EVERYBODY HAS THEIR OWN SOUND

Music/Lyrics by Jerry Brodey
© 1992 JERRY BRODEY (Socan)

CHORUS:
Everybody has their own sound
Unique, with character — a sound
It's a la la la (repeat)
It's a ho ho ho (repeat)
It's ca va bien! (repeat)
It's anagaseo (repeat)

Everybody has their own sound
It could be language, a feeling, cry, or tee hee hee
Everybody's got it,
It's a similarity.

(chorus)

It's a baby's cry - WAAAAA!
It's a loving sigh - Mmmmm
It's a chuckle in your belly — laugh!
It's a way of saying hi — hello!

BRIDGE:
Everybody has their own sound
It could be the rhythmic way you jive,
Your walk, your talk;
It simply means that you're alive.

(chorus)

It's a yadee-daddy-da (repeat)
It's a hoty hoty who (repeat)
It's a grand to-do (repeat)
It's a ratta tatta ta (repeat)

Everybody has their own sound. (repeat)

EVERYBODY HAS THEIR OWN SOUND

Discussion

We are different in so many ways! Isn't it amazing how many unique faces, bodies, and personalities can be created. Even within one family, we can see sisters and brothers of greatly differing characteristics. In a whole classroom, diverse features abound. Talk about them:

What music do you listen to?
What is your favorite food?
What holidays do you celebrate?
What do you wear to dress up for a formal occasion?
What kind of dances do you know?
What languages do you know?
When is your birthday?
What TV shows do you like?
Do you sometimes prefer to be alone instead of with other people?
Do you prefer quiet or lots of noise?
What other individual characteristics can you think of?
In what ways are we similar?

Is it a problem that we are not all the same?
What would it be like if we were all the same?

Activities

1. WE ALL LOOK SPECIAL BOOK (All levels)

Have each child draw a self portrait, write their name and write about three things that make them feel good and three things that make them feel not so good. Put the pages together into a book. Then have students place their books on their desks and play musical chairs: As each child sits at every other child's desk, then write something nice about them.

2. PEOPLE COLLAGE (All levels)

Use magazines and newspaper photographs and illustrations to make a mural-sized people collage, showing faces of all descriptions.

The book "Anti-Bias Curriculum" from the National Association for the education of Young Children in Washington, D.C. has a wealth of ideas for teachers. It recommends the following for displays:

If the population of the class is predominately:

children of colour, more than half, although not all, of the images and materials in the environment should reflect their backgrounds in order to counter the predominance of white, dominant cultural images in the general society.

poor children (white and children of colour), a large number of images and materials should depict working-class life in all its variety in order to counter the dominant cultural image of middle- and upper-class life.

white children, at least one-half of the images should introduce diversity in order to counter the white-centred images of the dominant culture.

differently-abled children, they deserve learning about gender and cultural diversity as well as about the capabilities of people with special needs. A large number of images should depict children and adults with disabilities doing a range of activities.

If a few children are different from the rest of the group, then take care to ensure that those children's background is amply represented along with representations of the majority groups in the class.

3. GRAPHS (Grades 4 to 6)

Use math class to illustrate differences and similarities. Make a pie graph to show food preferences: how many students like tacos? pizza? egg rolls? perogies? matzo? Use a bar graph to show how many students have birthdays in each month of the year.

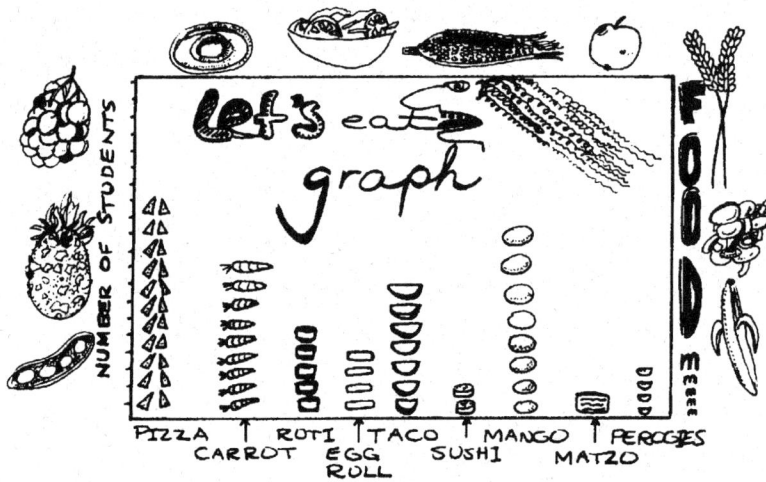

PINK AND BLUE

Why do boy babies wear blue?
Who started that rumour? Was it you?
And why do girl babies wear pink?
Who decided it, do you think?
Boys wear this, girls wear that,
Girls get dolls, boys get bats.
Do you think it's like that
Far across the sea?
Are blues and pinks used officially?

Is it in books?

Boys are adventurous, loud and tough,
Girls are dressed in frilly stuff.
Boys can hold a fist of worms
While gentle girls will stand and squirm.
It is so untrue!
How could each of us fit
In the very same shoe?

Is it on TV?

Little girls act the same way,
Caring for babies when they play;

Sharing secrets on the phone —
Should Ken call Barbie
When he comes home?
Little boys destroy towns —
With tanks and GI Joe around.

How can we peel back and crumple
these labels?
Deconstructing unfair fables.

There's confusion in the telecast.
My senses are in flabbergast!
Mom? Dad?
Will you get mad if I change the station,
Mixing colours, imagination?
Can I choose what I will be?
Finding out, who is ME.

So, if boy babies wear blue and girls
wear pink,
Switch them,
Blend them,
Now, what do you think?

PINK AND BLUE

Discussion

Listen to the poem Pink and Blue on the Can You Hear My Voice cassette before you have this discussion.

Has anybody not heard of the idea that pink is for girls and blue is for boys?

Where did the pink and blue "rules" come from?

Does everyone in the world attach the same meaning to pink and blue?

Where do people get their ideas about how boys and girls should act?

In your home, do the girls have certain chores that are different from the boys' chores?

Do the women do different chores from the men?

How do they decide who does what?

Can you think of other examples of things that are different for boys and girls?

What kind of toys do you receive for your birthday? Do your brothers and sisters receive the same types of toys?

Activities

1. SPECIAL DAYS (All levels)

To counteract the impact of male dominance in our society, make a point of celebrating special women's days whenever you can. International Women's Day, March 6, can be a chance to invite a special speaker to talk to the class about the accomplishments of women or about women's rights. On Mother's Day, honour the contributions of mothers to our society. Person's Day on Oct. 18 marks the day in 1929 that women were deemed eligible to become senators in Canada and thereby were officially recognized as persons.

2. GENDER STEREOTYPES (Kindergarten to Grade 3)
This idea is from the book "Anti-Bias Curriculum Tools For Empowering Young Children"

On facing pages glue a "fair" and an "unfair" picture about gender role, using pictures from magazines or photocopies of illustrations in books. An example of a "fair" picture is one that shows a classroom in which some girls and boys are playing with dolls, others with building blocks. An "unfair" or stereotypical picture might show a classroom in which all the girls are playing with dolls and all the boys with blocks.

Under each picture write a few sentences the children dictate about why they think a picture is fair or unfair. Build on this book as the year goes on. Read the book in the classroom and leave it where students can look at it by themselves.

3. OPPOSITE SEXES (Grades 4 to 6)
Have the boys write five reasons each why they would like and not like to be a girl and the girls write five reasons each why they would like and not like to be a boy. Then have the boys write five reasons why they like and don't like being a boy and the girls five reasons why they like and don't like being a girl. Compare and contrast the lists.

4. PHOTO ANALYSIS (Grades 4 to 6)
Students can work on this project in pairs. Each pair needs a newspaper, a photocopy of the worksheet (below) and some scrap paper for making notes. They should read the worksheet first and then go through the newspaper page by page, taking notes and then filling in the worksheet. When they have completed it, discuss the results:

How many pictures are of men and how many of women?
What are the different roles and occupations of the men and women pictured?
What do these figures imply?
What is the representation of people of different racial groups?
Is that fair?
How many children are pictured compared to adults?
Why do you think this is?
How many seniors are pictured?
How many physically challenged people are pictured?
Do these results accurately reflect a day in the city?
Who decides what pictures to put in the paper?
Do you think the paper is geared to a certain group of readers?

PHOTO ANALYSIS WORKSHEET

Count all the people in the pictures whose faces are at least as big as a quarter.

How many people are pictured in the paper? _____

How many are men? _____

What are the occupations or roles of the men? (examples: politicians, business leaders, officials from organizations, athletes, criminals, models) _____
_____

How many are women?_____

What are the occupations or roles of the women (use the same examples as above)? _____
_____

How many are people of colour? _____

How many are not people of colour? _____

How many are children? _____

How many are not children? _____

How many are seniors? _____

How many are physically challenged? _____

ROCKY ROAD

New Lyrics by Jerry Brodey and Ken Whiteley
© 1992 (Socan)

Our road goes up, our road goes down
Sing marley charley call you.
Sometimes it's level on the ground
Sing marley charley call you.

CHORUS:
Right through, right through the rocky road
Sing marley charley call you. (repeat)

There's a place I want to go,
Sing marley charley call you.
How I get there I don't know.
Sing marley charley call you.

(chorus)

I can stand alone or stand with friends,
Sing marley charley call you.
I'll keep on standing till the end
Sing marley charley call you.

(chorus)

Food for my plate, drink for my cup,
Sing marley charley call you.
This song to lift my spirits up.
Sing marley charley call you.

(chorus)

Traditional, Jamaican

ROCKY ROAD

Discussion

When our life journeys take us over some rocky patches in the road it can be helpful to know how to co-operate and work together. Discuss:

How do you ask for help when you need it?
Are most people happy to help or not?
Do you like it when someone helps you?
Has anyone ever asked you for help with something?
Did you like helping?
Have you ever been afraid to ask for help from someone? why?
What are some things you like to do with others but not by yourself?
What are some things you like to be alone to do?

Activities

1. JAMAICAN DANCE
(Kindergarden to Grade 3)

In Jamaica, some children dance like this while they sing a version of Rocky Road: Form two facing lines. Link hands with the partner across from you and form an arch over the rocky road below. Throughout the choruses, couples dance underneath the arches to the opposite ends of the lines. During the verses knees bend and arches sway in time to the music.

2. ROCKY ROAD BOARD GAME (Grades 4 to 6)

In this co-operative game, children work together to avoid obstacles on the way home from school. If they help each other pass the tough spots without losing anyone along the way, and arrive home before time is up, they win!

Six to eight children can play at a time, so divide the class into four or five groups so each group can make its own game set.

Use a fairly large piece of cardboard for the board so the whole team can sit around it comfortably. Draw a winding path from one corner to the diagonally opposite corner, trying to cover as much of the board as possible with curves and twists en route. In board-game fashion, make the path of large square blocks. There should be about 100 squares, each one a step on the way home.

Call one corner School – this is the start position. The other corner is Home. Fill in 6 of the squares along the way with hazards – things that can slow you down – such as the following:

forgot math book at school – need 1 buddy to go back and get it
bullies pick on you – need 4 helpers
an unknown driver asks if you want a ride home - team must
gather and phone an adult (1 quarter)
stuck in the corner store – need 1 friend to move on
lost house key – need quarter to call a friend
tripped and fell – need quarter for a bandaid

In addition to the board, you need: a marker for each player on the team, a die, four fake quarters, six blank squares, a timer.

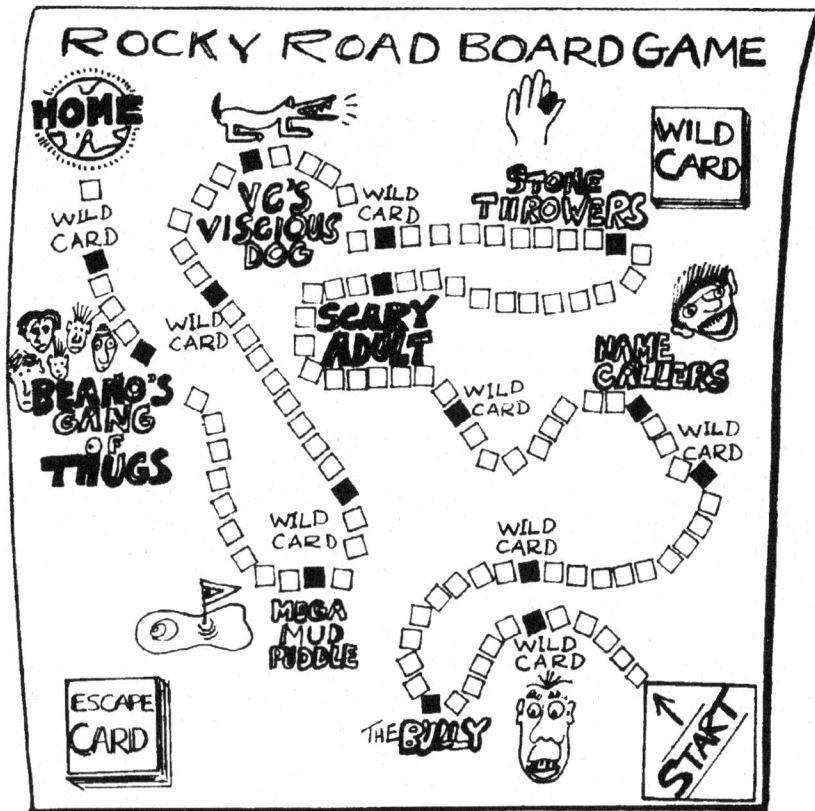

ROCKY ROAD BOARD GAME

To play:

Set the timer to an agreed length of time. Roll to see who goes first – high roll is first.

In turn, players roll the die and move their markers that number of blocks. If they land on a "quarter" they hold onto it – they may need it. If they land on a hazard, they are stuck until the requirement on the hazard is met.

Players who forget their math book must wait for another player to move back or forward to that square and together they must return to the school and start again. If a player is faced with bullies, four other players must use their turns to roll back to that square to help out. Players will have to discuss between them who is the best suited to help out in each case.

Once the conditions of the hazard have been met, cover that hazard with a blank square so other players don't run into it.

To win the game, all players must arrive home before the time is up.

Have students illustrate their game boards using paint, markers, plastiscine for hills, little model homes and stores and anything they want. Encourage them to add new hazards or change old ones if they have better ideas. The rules are flexible, too – if they think of a different way to play, as long as it is co-operative, so much the better!

3. ONLY ONE CANOE (Grades 4 to 6)

We saw a very successful version of this activity performed by the Théâtre de la Marmaille at an international children's festival.

Before you start, have a discussion about the stages of life: Children are our hope for the future; young adults have the strength and energy to provide for society; older people contribute the wisdom of experience. In what other ways do we enrich our society at different ages? Do our rights differ at different ages?

Divide the class into two or three groups. Assign a "character" to each group member, aiming for a fairly even distribution of elderly men and women, middle-aged men and women, girls and boys, and girl and boy babies. Try to give girls the male parts and boys the female parts.

Tell the groups they are marooned on a desert island with only one canoe to take them to safety. The canoe can hold three people at a time (four if one is a baby) and the trip to safety will take four days. What should the group do?

The object is to demonstrate that males and females of every age group are important; one is not more valuable than another. Attempting to rescue the marooned islanders by canoe might lead to students deciding that one group is more worth saving than another. Can they justify this? The group discussions may bring up individuals' biases for or against certain age groups or sexes. Encourage characters in different age groups to defend themselves and each other against being left behind. Is escaping the only solution?

Have each group report their survival ideas to the class when they are finished. Have students write a paper on what they personally thought about the exercise.

WALK IN SOMEONE ELSE'S SHOES

Music/Lyrics by Jerry Brodey
© 1992 JERRY BRODEY (Socan)

CHORUS:
Sometimes you can't understand
Another person's blues.
Unless you see what it's like
For yourself
To walk in someone else's shoes.

What if I didn't have eyes to see.
Would I mind somebody directing me?
How could I know about the smiles you wear?
I'd feel the force of your stare.

(chorus)

What if I lived far away
Where people didn't look like me?
Would I be treated the same? Called some name?
Asked to go back home from where I came?

What if I were Grandmother May
Taken quick to a nursing home.
How would it feel not to be free?
She was so used to living on her own.

(chorus)

There are times I've been mad,
'Cause I don't have things that others have.
What can anybody do unless they step in my shoes
To really know how I feel the blues.

WALK IN SOMEONE ELSE'S SHOES

Discussion

Listen to Walk In Someone Else's Shoes together and discuss the idea of imagining other people's feelings. For children in some situations, for example those who are particularly close to elderly grandparents or those who are recent immigrants, this discussion might touch a tender nerve.

What would it be like to be blind?
Does anyone know a blind person?
How is their life different?
Has anyone ever been in a far-away country?
Can you imagine being in a place where nobody speaks your language?
Has anyone visited a nursing home?
What do you think elderly people like about nursing homes?
What do you think they don't like?
Would you like to live in a nursing home when you are older?
Where else could elderly people live?
Have you ever felt bad because you don't have what others have ?
Have you ever felt good for someone else?

Activities

1. OUTREACH/INREACH (All levels)

Use the resources of your neighbourhood to introduce students to people of different ages and abilities. If there is a senior citizens home nearby, talk with the program director about ways your students can interact with the residents. Perhaps your Grade 6 class could tape record and later write down stories the seniors have of the neighbourhood in earlier years. Your Kindergarten class could visit the home, in costume, on Halloween. (Don't assume the seniors all want to mix with younger people. Some prefer their privacy.)

Invite differently-abled people to speak to your class about their experiences. Students can learn about how hearing-impaired people talk on the telephone, how a sightless person repairs bicycles, or how an art student in a wheel chair gets around the art college.

2. STORYTELLING (Kindergarten to Grade 3)

There are many ways to explain to children that their version of any situation is not the only version. One teacher we know collects folk tales from around the world to read to her primary students. Invariably, the students recognize the same stories told with slight variations, depending on the origins of the version.

3. DIZZY SPELL (Grades 4 to 6)

Here's an exercise to try during gym class (some students might not be physically able to do this). Have students hold onto a metre-stick and then, keeping their eyes on the stick, spin around 10 times as fast as they can. Drop the stick and try to walk in a straight line. How do they feel? Tell them that this is how some stroke victims feel all the time.

Another way to imagine the daily frustrations that face some differently-abled people is to have right-handed students use only their left hand for 10 minutes and left-handed students use only their right.

4. COOKIE SHARING (Grades 4 to 6)

This activity is a good opportunity to introduce concepts of class differences as they apply to unequal distribution of wealth on which much racism is patterned.

Two students in the class receive five cookies each.

Seventeen students receive one cookie each.

Six students receive one cookie to share between them.

Students quickly grasp the unfairness of this arrangement. Talk about it in a global sense. How did the third group of children feel about having to share a cookie?

5. WRITING FROM A NEW VIEW (Grades 4 to 6)

Have students re-write a folk tale from the point of view of one of the "misunderstood" characters. How do you think the wolf felt in the three pigs story? The step-sisters in Cinderella?

Or, instead of using folk tales, use this as an exercise for a novel students are reading for language. Have them identify the antagonist in the story and summarize how he or she might have felt.

Another way to try to imagine an alternate perspective is to write a story about a child living on a desert island. The inhabitants of this small tropical island speak dolphin language but no human language, and they have no knowledge of modern technology. One day, some Canadians come to the island by airplane and the child is taken to Canada. What happens to her there?

WHAT WOULD IT BE LIKE

Lyrics by Grade 6 — 9 students from Walter Whyte School,
Grand Marais, Manitoba / Music by Victoria Moon Joyce.
© 1992 Socan

CHORUS:
What would it be like?
A world without war,
Where people can relate.
And learn to love a little more.

In every person's loving heart
There's a potential for war.
It can tear your life apart
Trying to settle other scores.

(chorus)

When your world is in confusion
Peace seems only an illusion.
There comes a time when each of us,
Must believe there's a solution.

(chorus)

BRIDGE:
And after all our tears
Have washed away our grief.
Turn our face toward the years —
Hoping for a lasting peace.

When your mind gets torn and rattled
Like a hurricane at sea.
You may choose to join the struggle to make peace,
Before our spirit can be free.

(chorus)

Learn to listen a little more,
Learn to give a little more,
Learn to love a little more.

WHAT WOULD IT BE LIKE?

Discussion

This song was written by Moon Joyce and students in Grades 6 to 9 at Walter Whyte School in Grand Marais, Manitoba. It asks what it would be like to live in a world where there is no war. Listen to the song on the cassette and discuss:

Who uses weapons?

For what purposes?

Can conflict be solved without war?

Is conflict always violent?

Is there anything wrong with conflict?

Do you ever see conflict at school? at home? on TV? at the movies?

Do you think it's dangerous to joke about violence?

Do you think violent cartoons incite violence?

Do you ever see conflict solved without violence at home or on TV?

Are there times when you have not felt safe?

What does safety feel like?

What does safety look like?

Are weapons necessary for safety?

What is power?

Who has it?

Name some situations where you see power being used inappropriately and appropriately

Activities

1. PEACEMAKING (All levels)

Downtown Alternative School in Toronto has successfully adapted a conflict management program through which students, called peacemakers, mediate everyday school-yard conflicts.

First, the peacemakers ask the children in conflict if they want the teacher to be called or if they would like to try peace-making. If so, the peacemakers explain the rules: No interruptions. No running away. No name calling. No plugging your ears. Tell the truth.

Then, in turn, the children in conflict listen to each other tell their stories of what happened. The peacemakers ask: Is that all you have to say? The peacemakers might be required to state the problem, making sure not to lay any blame. Suggestions for solutions are asked for until one is found that all can agree on.

The children have found it is fairest when peacemakers work in pairs. The rules are flexible enough to evolve over time. Sometimes the peacemakers can't help and the case is referred to a teacher. Other times all that was needed was to clear the air and a solution is not required at all. Sometimes peacemaking has to wait until both participants have cooled off.

To find out more about peacemaking, read the resources guide at the end of this book.

2. NEW ENDINGS (Grades 4 to 6)

Many television programs for children include violent solutions to problems. Have one or two children recap a recent episode of, for example, Teenage Mutant Ninja Turtles. Divide the class into groups of three or four and ask each group to come up with a way to end the program that is co-operative instead of violent. Have each group present their new endings to the class, and discuss. Why did the television writer choose the violent ending instead of the co-operative ending?

3. ROLE PLAYING (Grades 4 to 6)

When children fight, it's often because they don't know how to solve their disagreements any other way. One safe way of experimenting with different methods of problem solving is to role play. Divide the class into groups of four or five students and have each group select a scenario from the list below.

First each group (make sure everyone participates) acts out the scene as it is written. Allow a maximum of one minute for this and then clap hands three times to "freeze" the action.

Ask students to brainstorm about the scene. How did each character feel? Why did they feel that way? What could have happened to change these feelings? Allow 10 minutes for discussion and then have students re-enact the scenario showing a way it could have been handled better.

Discuss the solution. Do students have other ideas?

Here are some ideas for scenarios:

1. A child passes out birthday party invitations to everyone in the group except one. The children who receive invitations huddle together excitedly, talking about the party. The one who was left out is isolated and begins to cry.

2. One of the children is given a nickname, The Brainer. He or she doesn't like the nickname and tries to tell the others but they don't listen.

3. A child comes to school with an expensive new toy. The other children fight over it and it is broken. Everybody yells at the child who broke it.

4. A child's aging grandmother comes to the classroom to deliver his or her lunch. The other children tease the grandchild

5. A child is having difficulty learning to read, often reversing words in a sentence. Another child is the best reader in the class. The good reader brags to the learner and classmates laugh. The learner becomes angry.

> As much as possible during role-plays, have boys act girl characters and girls act boy characters to help them develop an understanding of each other.

SOBONANA KUSASA
(We Will Meet Tomorrow)

Music/Lyrics by Jerry Brodey
© 1980 JERRY BRODEY (Socan)

Zulu language

1. *Sobonana Kusasa (repeat)*
   Sobonana Kusasa (repeat)
   Sobo (repeat)
   Nana (repeat)
   Ku (repeat)
   Sasa (repeat)

2. *Sobanana Kusasa che che che*

3. *Sobonana Kusasa che che che eh!*

4. *We will meet to-morrow*

5. *Sobonana Kusasa*

SOBONANA KUSASA

Discussion

This song is in Zulu, a language from South Africa. Discuss:
Who decides that English and French are Canada's official languages?
What impact does that have on people who speak other languages?
What would happen if everybody spoke their own language?
What would happen if everybody spoke one language?
Who decides what holidays are national holidays?
What impact does that have on people who celebrate other holidays?
What are the special days that you and your family celebrate?
Why are these days important?

Activities

1. HELLO-GOODBYE POSTER (All levels)

Make a poster for the classroom that shows how to say hello and goodbye in as many languages as possible. You could make it using a map to pinpoint where the different languages come from. Every morning greet the class with a hello from a different language. Every afternoon, say a different goodbye. If this is a multicultural classroom, have a map showing countries of origin of different students.

2. MULTICULTURAL CALENDAR (All levels)

Did you know that in Dhaka, Bangladesh, the daily newspaper has three different dates on it? One is according to the Gregorian calendar used in Canada, the second is the Hindu date and the third is the Muslim date, which uses a lunar calendar.

Make sure your classroom calendar notes the dates of occasions important to all the members of your class – and more. Explain the significance of the dates at the beginning of the years and, as they occur, honour the traditions appropriately.

> Educators warn against teaching a "tourist curriculum." The book Anti-Bias Curriculum defines trivializing as organizing activities only around holidays or only around food. Reading books about children of colour only on special occasions, it says, disconnects cultural diversity from daily classroom life.

3. CHILDREN'S DAY (All levels)

Caroline Parry's excellent multicultural resource book "Let's Celebrate!" tells us that Tibetan Buddhists in Canada have begun to observe Children's Day on Dec. 25. "A special home shrine is set up and covered in silk. All the children in the family collect the objects that mean the most to them and arrange them on this shrine. They are given presents of dolls or figures of inspiring people to place on the shrine. Parents and other adults all celebrate the children in their lives on this day."

How would your class celebrate Children's Day? Design a celebration that recognizes children around the world. Pick a date and have a celebration!

4. ALPHABETS (Grades 4 to 6)

Display different alphabets and writing systems, for example Russian, Cree, Braille, Hebrew, Chinese, Thai and so on. Label materials in more than one language. Invite children to write their names in different languages. Teach them how to say their name in sign language and how to write it in Braille.

5. IDIOMS (Grades 4 to 6)

There are many different ways of speaking English – we all have accents. Think of English as it is spoken in Australia, New Orleans, Newfoundland, Honk Kong, Pakistan, and some Caribbean countries. It is ethnocentric to refer to one form of English as "the norm" and other versions as "substandard".

Make a dictionary of idioms, including entries from as many different regions as possible. (And don't forget to include your own region. You use expressions that are not familiar in other places.) Here are some examples to get started:

boot:	trunk of a car (England)
lollie:	candy (Australia)
pocketbook:	purse (U.S.)
plats:	braids (Australia)

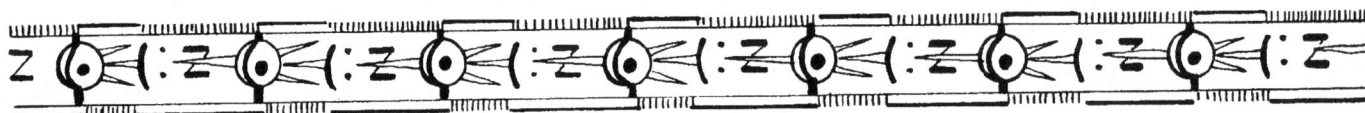

GUIDELINES FOR EQUALITY IN THE CLASSROOM

PROVIDE an inclusive curriculum. Display images that reflect a variety of cultures, ages and abilities. Make sure to have a balance of pictures of boys and girls, abled and differently abled people, whites and people of colour. Choose books that represent social values, attitudes and historical information about a diversity of cultures.

SET LIMITS to stop discriminatory behaviour in the classroom. Make it a firm rule that no aspect of a person's identity – gender, race, ethnicity, disability, religion, class – is ever an acceptable reason for exclusion or teasing.

DON'T IGNORE or evade questions about racial characteristics. Encourage children to ask about themselves and others by answering in a matter-of-fact, accurate way, appropriate to age level. If necessary, explain that you need time to answer the question, and then do some research. Your board's race relations consultant should be able to help you.

GUARD AGAINST exhibiting unconscious biases. Most of us are not intentionally racist or sexist, but we all have built-in biases. Prejudice is woven into the fabric of our society. Do you unconsciously allow boys more time to talk than girls? Do you compliment girls on appearance and boys on achievement or tolerate aggressive behaviour in boys more than in girls? Do you have higher expectations for white children than for children of colour?

ACKNOWLEDGE differences in physical abilities. Saying that a hearing-impaired child is "just like you" to a child who can hear is confusing and doesn't give either child the information they need to play with each other. Help both children see how they are different and how they are the same.

BEWARE of ethnocentrism – a tendency to view groups or cultures in terms of one's own. It is ethnocentric to apply words such as backward or uncivilized to people whose culture values oral tradition over written tradition, for example. It is ethnocentric to refer to India (which is west of Japan) as the Far East.

BELIEVE that people will change. Much racist or sexist behaviour is unconscious and unintentional. Helping children understand the harmful consequences of their actions will often lead to changed attitudes and new behaviour.

REMEMBER, we make mistakes and we can't be "politically" correct all the time. Have a sense of humour about yourself and others. If you don't know how to deal with a situation immediately, it can wait. Take time to think it over or, if possible, consult a resource person and then address the issue again.

GLOSSARY

ANTI-SEMITISM is an attitude, belief or feeling that results in and helps to justify unfair treatment of Jews.

BIAS is a positive or negative feeling toward a group. Bias may be based on conscious theory or articulated stereotypes or it may be a totally unconscious preference for one group rather than others.

CLASSISM assumes and enforces the legitimacy, power and values of a particular group of people – in our society the middle and upper classes. Class barriers to equality may be subtly manifested at school, for example, when teachers ask students about vacations and trips, assuming all children have these experiences. Stories about people who succeed because of hard work send a confusing message to a child whose parents are struggling very hard and not making it.[1]

DISCRIMINATION happens when prejudice is combined with action. Discrimination can be either overt or covert, conscious or unconscious, but one way or another it involves preferential treatment of a certain group, exclusion of others.

ETHNOCENTRISM is a tendency to view alien groups or cultures in terms of one's own and the belief in the inherent superiority of one's own group and culture, accompanied by a feeling of contempt for other groups and cultures.[2]

HANDICAPPISM is any attitude, action or institutional practice that subordinates people due to their disability. Handicappist institutional practices prevent the integration of disabled people into the mainstream of society and keep them socially and economically oppressed.[3]

HOMOPHOBIA is a fear and hatred of gay men and lesbians.

MULTICULTURALISM is a sharing of cultures. It empowers individuals who then share that strength among groups. It expands cultural consciousness into global consciousness.[4]

PREJUDICE is an opinion about a person or group of people formed without knowledge.

RACISM is an attitude, action or practice that subordinates people because of their colour.

SEXISM is an attitude, action or practice that subordinates people because of their sex.

A STEREOTYPE is an oversimplified picture that attributes a particular quality to all members of a group – rock stars are junkies, athletes are stupid, business people are greedy. Stereotypes freeze individuals into categories which deny their individuality and set up false expectations.[5]

1   from Open Minds to Equality – A Sourcebook for Learning Activities to Promote Race, Sex, Class and Age Equity
2   from Cultural Etiquette – A Guide for the Well-Intentioned
3   from Anti-Bias Curriculum – Tools for Empowering Young Children
4   from Globalchild – Multicultural Resources for Young Children
5   from Anti-Racist Education and the Adult Learner, The Board of Education for the City of Toronto

RESOURCES

Ball, Gerry and Palomares, Uvaldo. Grounds for Growth – The Human Development Program's Comprehensive Theory, Human Development Training Institute, San Diego, Calif.

Cech, Maureen. Globalchild – Multicultural Resources for Young Children, Ottawa: Health and Welfare Canada 1990

Crippen, Carolyn. The Magic Circle, FWTAO Newsletter, December, 1990/January 1991

Derman Sparks, Louise and the A.B.C. Task Force. Anti-Bias Curriculum – Tools for Empowering Young Children, National Association for the Education of Young Children, Washington, D.C., 1989

Fine, Esther; Lacey, Ann; Baer, Joan and Rother, Barbara. Children as Peacemakers, FWTAO Newsletter, December 1991/January 1992

Katz, Judith H. White Awareness – Handbook for Anti-Racism Training, University of Oklahoma Press, 1978

Kreidler, William J. Creative Conflict Resolution – Activities for Keeping Peace in the Classroom K-6, Scott, Foresman & Co.

Muzumdar, Pria and Saddiqui, Yasmeen. FUNCEPTS, producing workshops for students and teachers on racial diversity. 98 Gothic Ave. Toronto, Ont. M6P 2V9 (416) 766-8185

National Film Board of Canada. Playing Fair, series order # C9191 131 (a series of discussion-starters about racism, respect and equality for children 7 to 12)

Parry, Caroline. Let's Celebrate! Kids Can Press Ltd., Toronto, 1987

Schniedewind, Nancy and Davidson, Ellen. Open minds to Equality – A Sourcebook of Learning Activities to Promote Race, Sex, Class and Age Equity, Allyn and Bacon, 1983

Students at Downtown Alternative School, Toronto. The Peaceosaurus

The Board of Education for the City of Toronto. Anti-Racist Education and the Adult Learner – A Handbook for Educators in Adult and Continuing Education Programs, Toronto Board of Education, 1991

Three Rivers, Amoja. Cultural Etiquette – A Guide for the Well-Intentioned, 1990. Distributed by Market Wimmin, Box 28, Indian Valley, VA 24105

Kim and Jerry Brodey *have performed their music for thousands of children, parents and teachers across Canada and the United States. They share an impressive background as performers, educators, writers and workshop facilitators committed to cultural enhancement of school aged children. Kim and Jerry are heavily involved in developing, writing and performing curriculum packages which include practical activities to help teachers create a vision for social activism with their students.*

Ruth-Ann MacKinnon *is a mother, writer and editor who has lived and travelled in eastern and western Canada and U.S., South America, Europe and Asia. She shares Kim and Jerry's passion for social justice and their optimism that we can evolve a more caring society.*

Can You Hear My Voice (1992) Cassette
Can You Hear My Voice is a colourful blend of original songs and poetry with an upbeat feel. It encourages us to step into each other's shoes and listen to each other's stories. The songs promote respect and appreciation for the many ways we look, feel and act.

Let's Help This Planet (1991) Cassette, Songbook, Teachers' Guide
This cassette is a musical adventure into our environment...and more. The Brodeys use lots of humour and musical styles to sing their way through our oceans, rainforests, orchards and villages right back home. Along the way we meet lions and mice and discover the importance of giving back to our precious mother earth.

The songbook is a wonderful companion to the cassette with lyrics, simple piano arrangements and guitar chords for each song on the cassette plus two more songs from the *Out Of This World* recording — *Boat Goes Down The River* and *Walking Through The Jungle.*

The Teachers' Guide is a complement to the cassette. Song by song it offers many fun activities (Grades K-6) which will help students become active earthkeepers. All the ideas in the book are linked to other areas like reading, writing, math, geography and science.

Out Of This World (1989)
Kim and Jerry and their band The Leapin' Lizards blend their superb harmonies with theatrical playfulness in this music extravaganza. Favourites such as *Holes in My Imagination, Jump Up, Boat Goes Down the River* and *Walking Through the Jungle* offer listeners a memorable dance into the imagination.

Family Pie (1986)
Family Pie received a Notable Recording award by the American Library Association and was also nominated for a Juno (for Best Children's Recording) by colleagues in the recording industry. Kim and Jerry sing about universal themes and empowerment. *Let's Help This Planet, This is My Family* and *Walking to Freedom* are thought-provoking songs dealing with our environment, different families, and the difficult subjects of racism.

Hats On/Hats Off (1986), a 30 minute WHITMAN/GOLDEN Video
Kim and Jerry's first video is highly entertaining and accessible to family members 3-11 years old. This video is a winner of the Action for Children Television Award for "responsible children's programming." Songs included are *There Is A Robot, Melting All My Cares, 3-6-9 (The Goose Drank Wine), When You're In The Bedroom, Going To Toronto* and *Garbage No, No, No.*

Simple Magic (1984)
This very popular recording was nominated for an American Library Notable Recording and Parent's Choice Ward. There is traditional material such as *My Bonnie, Pop Goes The Weasel, Going To Toronto, Vive L'Amour* and *Shortnin' Bread.* Jerry has penned some of the duo's most requested songs: *When You're In The Bedroom, The Captain and Me* and *There Is A Robot.*

Carnival (1982)
This is Jerry's second solo recording. It is a wonderful collection of songs spanning different cultures ideas from Senegal to Jamaica to our own backyard. The old nugget *Side by Side* and schoolyard favourite *3-6-9 (The Goose Drank Wine)* are delightful. Sample some of Jerry's best songwriting — *Flying Through Space, Chante* and *Carnival.*

Professional Development Workshops

Kim and Jerry Brodey
offer these
workshops and keynote concerts

Let's Help This Planet

In this highly-participatory workshop Kim and Jerry creatively explore enduring environmental issues such as waste disposal, global education and resource conservation. Workshop participants play with environmental music, poetry and prose and return to the classroom with ready-to-use ideas.

Size of Group: 15-45   Length: 2 1/2 hours

Let's Help This Planet - concert

Kim and Jerry perform their hugely successful school concert as keynote for environmental science and music conferences.

Length: 55 minutes

Creative Words and Music

Kim and Jerry present a fresh but systematic approach to exploring music and whole language and building self-esteem. Participants are led through a variety of creative, hands-on exercises that reinforce musical concepts first individually and then in small co-operative groups. Kim and Jerry take a close look at how to integrate special themes such as multiculturalism with music.

Size of Group: 15-45   Length: 2 1/2 hours

Can You Hear My Voice

Using music, art and drama this challenging workshop offers dozens of classroom activities which encourage communication, self-esteem, pride on our respective cultures, language and ethnic backgrounds. It promotes respect and appreciation for the many ways we look, feel and act.

Size of Group: 15-20   Length: Half or full day